MA, BSc, A

Max Eggert firs e transferring his a from there to Industria stminster and recently to clinical work at Sheffield University.

He enjoyed a successful career in HR and General Management but was fired in 1983 after appearing on the Money Programme. His career then really took off as a Management Consultant and he has worked with many thousands of people as a trainer or advisor in the UK, US and Australia. He is currently managing partner of Transcareer, an international consultancy dedicated to the empowerment of people at work. He works mainly in the UK and Australia as a strategist and as an advisor to organizations as well as a counsellor.

Max has two adult children, lives in Gateshead and Sydney and has a consuming passion for riding. His current research interest is in clinical hypnosis for career development. As a priest, he also works in the dioceses of Chichester and Sydney as an N.S.M.

Other titles by Max Eggert
published by Arrow Books

The Perfect CV

The Perfect Interview

The Perfect Career

The Perfect Consultant (with Elaine van der Zeil)

THE BOOK OF *Career Questions*

Two hundred plus questions that will change the whole of your working life

Max Eggert

Arrow Books Limited 1996

1 3 5 7 9 10 8 6 4 2

Arrow Books Limited
20, Vauxhall Bridge Road, London SW1V 2SA

Random house Australia (Pty) Limited
PO Box 337, Bergvlei, south Africa

Random House UK Limited Reg. No. 954009

Papers used by Random house UK Ltd are natural, recyclable products made from wood grown in sustainable forests. The manufacturing processes conform to the environmental regulations of the country of origin.

Companies, institutions and other orgaizations wishing to make bulk purchases of any business books published by Random House should contact their local bookstore or Random House direct:
Special Sales Director, Random House,
20 Vauxhall Bridge Road, London SW1V 2SA
Tel: 0171 973 9670 Fax: 0171 828 6681

Random House UK Ltd Limited Reg. No. 954009

ISBN 0 09 964871 7

Printed and bound in Great Britain by
Cox & Wyman Ltd, Reading, Berks.

For
Heather Ann
Marisian Clare
and Gillian

who ask me more questions than
I could ever answer

ACKNOWLEDGEMENTS

Heather Weatherstone	– for her continual encouragement and support as my partner.
Fokkina McDonnell	– for at least 30 of these questions, encouragement and ideas.
Ros Tovey	– for word processing support and coping with my dyslexia.
Elizabeth Hennessy	– for being patient and not harassing me when I lost one script in Australia and the other was stolen from my car in Leeds.
Michael Millard	– for going over the proofs and making valuable suggestions

And all my clients, both corporate and individual, with whom it has been a pleasure to work and from whom I have learnt much.

Note: In this book he/she are interchangeable.

INTRODUCTION

At General Motors it used to be said

'Be loyal to the company and the company will be loyal to you.'

But such days are over. Responsibility for work and career now falls to you to look after yourself.

This little book just asks questions, but if you work through them – preferably pondering your thoughts first before marshalling your ideas and writing down your answers – you will find that the way you work and what you do will change. Your work will take on a new perspective.

In my experience most people are in what I call 'career drift', that is others are in control of their working lives in terms of both content and direction. Those I know who are both successful and inordinately happy with their careers march to their own drum along life's highway. Successful people take responsibility for their successes and learn from their failures. For many it is not until they are fired or made redundant that they realise that work, however enjoyable, is but a contractual relationship and there are few obligations an employer has towards those who have worked so hard and so faithfully.

If I were a luckier person maybe I would believe in luck for career but most successful people have usually made their own luck and ensured they stood where the face of good fortune could smile upon them.

If you hope for luck or good fortune to transform your lot in life then the questions are not for you.

Thank you for purchasing this little book and I trust that in some way your work becomes your passion and that you become the master or mistress of your own career.

Max A Eggert
Rushcutters Bay
Sydney, NSW
July 1995

'Just do it'

Nike advertisement

THE FIVE MOST POWERFUL CAREER QUESTIONS

1. What work would you do if you only had twelve months to live? (Assume you must work and that you enjoy good health until the moment of your death.)

2. What work would you do for the next ten years if you won millions on the lottery? (Assume that you must continue to work.)

3. What one job would you do if you knew you could not fail?

4. In the world of work, whom do you most admire and would like to emulate?

5. Looking back over the whole of your career to date, when have you been really happy and contented? Why?

200 VITAL CAREER QUESTIONS

1. What do you like about your present job and what does that tell you about what you should be doing in the future?

2. What can you do now that you could not do:

   - a year ago?
   - five years ago?

   What were the circumstances around your new learning? Did you play an active part in your own development or did someone else decide for you?

3. Do you live to work or work to live?

4. How much do you

   - need to earn
   - want to earn
   - expect to earn

   when you reach the height of your career? Is it helpful for you to have financial goals?

5. When do you think you will reach your career peak? How old will you be? How will your life be different when you reach it?

6. Which organizations have the best reputation for the career you wish to pursue?

7. What has your organization done for your personal development recently?

8. When working with individuals what are you best at?
   When working with groups what are you best at?

9. In your work are you pro-active or reactive: are you driven by circumstances or do they drive you? How do you get things turned around and done?

10. Do you work harder for yourself than for other people? Is this right and what should you do about it? Is there such a thing as legitimate selfishness?

11. If you were offered a better job in another country would you take it or would you prefer to stay with your roots and your friends?

12. Whom in your organization do you admire or respect most? Why? How are you different from him or her? Should you emulate them in any way? What might be the result if you did?

13. In a team at work, do you prefer to work with men or women? Why? How does gender affect the way you work?

14. What aspect or incident in your career to date do you feel most ashamed of? Have you told or do you plan to tell anyone? What do you think their response might be? How are you going to prevent a recurrence?

15. What is the culture of your organization and how easily do your values sit within it? Is it important for you to feel 'at home' with your organization?

16. How do people at work know

- that you are happy?
- that you are pleased with them?
- that you admire them?
- that you wish they behaved differently?
- that you enjoy working with them?

17. What are you doing to maximize your profile

- in the office?
- in the unit?
- in the organization?
- in the industry?

18. Would you prefer to have a happy marriage or a happy career?

19. If you were once an alcoholic but have now been dry for five years, and during those years you managed to secure an executive position, would you take an alcoholic drink if:

- the chairman invited you to an exclusive executive cocktail party?
- an important client to the organization insisted?

20. What do you consciously do to strengthen your social network so that you might develop your career and advance yourself?

21. Your firm employs 250 people but is facing hard times and you have a choice of two strategies. The first would save 100 jobs, the other would save all the jobs, but this second option only has a 50% chance of success. Which would be your preference?

22. Could you ever be accused of being sycophantic to your boss (or to anyone else in a work context)?

23. What could you have done better at work

- today?
- this week?
- this month?
- this year?

What is it that brings about under-performance in yourself?

24. To whom do you go at work

- for moral support?
- to get advice?
- to help you solve a problem?
- for a loan?
- to give you honest feedback?
- to have fun with?

25. From your current job what are your most transferable skills? How might they help you in the future?

26. What would your current interests and the way you spend your disposable income tell a prospective employer about you?

27. What do you like least about your present job and what does that tell you about what you should be doing in the immediate and long-term future?

28. What have you done to develop your expertise in your present field in the past twelve months?

29. List your three greatest achievements at work. What does this tell you

- about your skills?
- your motivations?
- the work you should be pursuing?

30. Think of the last three people to be promoted in your organization – are there any common factors about them or their performance and what does this mean for you and the way you work?

31. How can you use your present job and organization to springboard to the next stage of your career?

32. If you were invited to apply for a position that you wanted, would you have your CV ready to fax immediately?

33. When on holiday

- what do you miss about your work?
- what do you not want to come back to?

34. What aspects of your job bore you?

35. Compare the golden moments of your life and of your career – what do they tell you about yourself, what are the common themes and what does this tell you about the future?

CAREER QUESTIONS

36. To become a consultant in the Health Service there is a door of opportunity which closes very slowly, but by the time you are forty years old it is usually quite firmly shut. What are the doors of opportunity in your chosen profession/career and what are you doing to pass through them or keep your doors open?

39. If you knew that you were going to be fired tomorrow, what example of your work would you like to take from the office?

40. Would you be happy if your child did the same job or followed the same career as you?

41. If you would like to improve or gain a special ability which would help your career, what would it be?

42. How often do you reward yourself for work well done? Would it motivate you more if you planned your rewards?

44. When and how do you avoid work that you don't want to do? Do you

- go in late or become sick?
- procrastinate?
- avoid people?

Why? And what should you be doing about it?

45. How much of your annual salary would you be prepared to invest in your own career development? How much have you spent so far this year?

46. Do you spend more time in social activities with your friends from work than with your children or with your partner? Is this the balance you really want?

47. If you were going to participate in an assessment centre for an important job or promotion and you discovered, innocently, which IQ test was going to be used during the assessment, would you endeavour to practise the test before the selection event in the hope of improving your scores?

48. If you knew your employer would go bankrupt in three years' time, how would this affect your current career plans and work behaviour?

49. How do you feel about friends who have been more successful than yourself in their careers so far?

50. How does your motivation and commitment to your present job compare with that of your colleagues?

51. What is the best thing you could be doing for your career

- today?
- this week?
- this month?
- this year?

52. When, ideally, should you be leaving your present job for the next one? What are you doing about your present plans?

53. Do you play an active part in your professional association? Would it help your career if you did?

54. What decisions at work do you find most difficult to make?

55. When you were a child, what did you want to do when you grew up? How close or otherwise have you come to your childhood dreams? What has brought about the difference between childhood ambition and adult reality?

56. With whom do you like to work?

57. If you were doing your ideal job, how differently would you behave? Would you be prepared to work for less money?

58. How much time do you spend on your personal development each week, how much should you be spending and what are you going to do about it?

59. In your job do you the right things or do things right? (Managers do the right things: leaders do things right.)

60. What sort of organization would you ideally like to work for? One that

- invents/makes and markets a product?
- provides a service to people?
- distributes information?
- is part of the public sector?
- is large or small?
- is local or international?

61. Where will you be in five years' time?

- what will you be doing?
- what will you have achieved?
- what will you be earning?

62. How many people do you know right now who might be able to offer you a job in the future? How many should you know?

63. In most James Bond movies the plot goes something like this: Bond is philandering, gets given mission impossible by 'M', is kitted out by 'Q', goes after Mr Big, finding beautiful girls along the way; having won the most beautiful he attacks Mr Big, there is a cataclysm, Mr Big escapes, as does Bond with the most beautiful girl and the film ends with 'M' being compromised by Bond's amorous exploits. This is the 'script' which being predictable makes Bond so popular. What are the scripts that run through your life?

64. Are you staying in the job to enjoy your successes or using your successes to springboard yourself to the next stage?

65. If your organization were offering voluntary redundancy with six months' net pay as a separation package, would you volunteer?

66. What advice would you give to your son and/or your daughter in their last year of education as they prepared themselves for the world of work?

67. In what way can you get your boss to support your career plans?

68. Are you a different person at work from what you are at home?

69. The Peter Principle suggests that everyone gets promoted to his or her level of incompetence – where do you think your level of incompetence will be and in what areas?

70. When did you last yell at someone or feel like yelling at someone at work? What are you going to do next time a similar situation arises?

71. What do your staff, colleagues or boss think are important to you from the way that you go about your work?

72. If your parents knew everything about your behaviour at work, would they be proud of you?

73. Would it matter to you who did your job if you left it? What aspects of your work would you like to continue after you leave?

74. Do you appraise others more or less by the stringent criteria and standards that you use for yourself?

75. If you wanted to do something at work and a colleague advised against it, would you still go ahead?

76. When you daydream at work – what do you think of most?

77. Do you prefer to work under pressure or in a calm and ordered environment?

78. What is your current market worth as an employee? How do you know? If it is above or below what you are currently receiving what are you/should you be doing about it?

79. Are you physically fit enough to do what you want to do?

80. If your career was a play or a film, how is it going to end? How would you like it to end?

81. Why did you buy this book?

82. Who in your current organization can be most helpful to you to develop your career in the directions you wish to go? How could you improve your relationship with them?

83. On a scale of 1 to 10, with 10 being the highest how hard are you working compared with:

- your colleagues?
- your capacity?

84. What special gifts do you bring personally to your job?

85. How often do you review your career progress, and is that time span still appropriate?

86. If you did not go back to work what would you be remembered for?

87. Which meetings should you be attending to ensure you have maximum profile?

88. What risks have you taken in your career, and what has been the pay off? What risks have you taken recently? What is the next risk you should be taking? How can you maximize the likelihood of success?

89. How do you congratulate yourself and/or reward yourself for a job well done or for achieving a career milestone? If you don't reward yourself, who will?

90. If you were to change your sex suddenly how would that affect the way that you did your job?

91. Would you prefer to be ugly but successful in your career or good looking but unsuccessful in your work?

92. What are you doing to stay above office politics?

93. Do you find it easy to ask for support or help at work or do you soldier on by yourself?

94. Would you like your manager and colleagues to be really frank with you about your performance and behaviour at work or would you prefer not to know?

95. On a scale of 1 to 10, with 10 being the highest, how satisfied are you with your career progress to date? Why not 10? What plans have you to rectify the situation?

96. You are at a party with friends and your host begins to badmouth your organization and products or service: would you challenge your host?

97. What is the worst thing your boss could know about your work? About you?

98. Would you have an affair at work? Would it make a difference if:

- you were single?
- it was with the partner of your boss?
- it was with your boss?
- it was with a subordinate?
- it would considerably help your career?

99. What are your 'self-destruct' habits at work? What brings them about and what, if anything, do you want to do about them?

100. You have bought some expensive technical kit for the office and went over your budget. When you receive the invoice you find that you have not been charged for one of the items which was quite expensive. What would you do?

101. When at work have you made a big decision based upon intuition or 'gut feel' and what has been the result?

102. When you meet someone in a work context what impression do you want to create? Are you successful? How would you explain this?

103. How many head-hunters do you know? Which head-hunters specialize in your industry or sector?

104. Are you emotionally fit enough to do what you want to do?

105. How would your boss rate your future prospects?

106. What does your boss read professionally and should you be reading the same material?

107. Who has been the most influential person in your career to date? Should you have a similar mentor now?

108. If you had a reference what would it say and what would you like it to say?

109. Whom do you need to know to get on in your career?

110. What kind of person do you prefer to work with as your

- manager?
- colleague?
- subordinate?

111. Is it important for you to see the end results of your work?

112. What have been the happiest moments of your working life so far, and how could you engineer similar situations at work so you could enjoy the same moments again?

113. What would you have to do to make your boss more successful? What might be the benefits if you first did these things?

114. Good negotiators only ever negotiate from power – what power do you have and how might you increase it?

115. If you had to downsize your organization through a 10% reduction in headcount, what would be the criteria, in rank order, that you would set for the selection of those who would have to leave? Would your criteria make you a candidate for deselection?

116. If you had a magic wand (ie total executive control), what would you change:

- about yourself?
- about your performance?
- about your career to date?
- about your current job?
- about your current organization?

Why? What could you change if you really wanted to?

117. Do you prefer to work with people who are younger or older than yourself?

118. Would you or do you recruit people to work for you who are more able or less able than yourself?

119. Comparing yourself to the people you went to school with, how well do you think you have done and why? Is it of any significance?

120. If you discovered that the Chairman and Chief Executive of your organization were siphoning off money from the pension fund, what would you do:

- if you knew that blowing the whistle would ruin your career?
- if your actions were to be vindicated after five years?

121. Looking back over your career, in which period did you:

- achieve the most?
- enjoy the most?
- develop the most?

122. What has been your most embarrassing experience at work?

123. If you won the lottery, would you take a major shareholding in your firm?

124. In your career to date, whom have you influenced most?

125. What management development courses should you be putting yourself on?

126. Can you resist going with the group view even if your standards are compromised?

127. How many times have you been to the doctor in the last five years? How many times have you met with a Career Counsellor?

128. When was the last time you updated your referees on how your career has been developing?

129. On a scale of 1 to 10, how would you rate your chances of promotion and what can you do about improving your chances?

130. What do you spend your disposable income on? What does this tell you about your values, motivations and career interests?

131. Who in your organization has been most successful, how is your work behaviour different from that person's behaviour, and is it significant for what you want to do in the future?

132. If someone were to ask you to advise them on a career what would you say to them?

133. Who do you need to know to get on in your career?

134. What handicaps have you got that hamper your career – how have others similar to yourself overcome their difficulties?

135. Who do you need to impress to fulfil your current career aspirations?

136. Who do you need to impress to secure the promotion you want and how can you ensure that they hear/know of your good work?

137. The best sales people never run down their product, their colleagues, their company or even the competition – how do you stand on these items and what would be appropriate for you to do about it?

138. If you were fired this morning, which twenty people would you be phoning this afternoon, to tell them you are looking for the next stage of your career? (If you are an executive or director which fifty would you be calling?)

139. What would make a 'perfect day' at work for you? Why?

140. If a TV series were made about you and your work, what would be an appropriate theme song?

141. Who has helped you most in your career?

142. For your next promotion in the organization, who is your most likely competitor? Why? And what should you be doing about it?

143. Which is it better to have, a wild roller coaster of a career with lots of highs and lows or a steady bland career? (Assume total earnings are the same for both.)

144. Would you give up five years of your life if in return you achieved all your career goals?

145. How important is it to you that your organization should:

- behave ethically?
- be active in community affairs?
- act in a 'green' way?
- operate the spirit of an equal opportunities programme?
- have a positive discrimination policy?

146. Do you prefer to be overdressed or underdressed at work? Do you dress more like top management or like those in the more humble positions?

147. What sort of boss would you have to have to bring the very best out in you?

148. Do you find it easy to take advice about work problems? Do you actively seek it? On what subjects? Who would you go to?

149. If you were dismissed today, how long would your finances last at your current standard of living?

150. If you had a motto for yourself at work, what would it be?

151. What made you choose the career you are now in? Do those factors still apply today?

152. What sort of person do you work with best and why?

153. Who have been your work role models in the past?

154. What could you do to make your job more enjoyable and fun

- for yourself?
- for your team?

155. What formal qualifications or courses do you need to achieve your career peak and when are you going to get them?

156. Are changes in your life brought about by:

- others?
- the expectation of success?
- failure?
- pain?

157. What are your unique skills? (Identify six and give two examples from work to prove each of them.)

158. How much time do you spend at work working on your work objectives and how much on your personal career objectives, and how are you going to get the balance right?

159. It is said that credit is always available at the bank when you are rich enough not to need it. When is it better to network? When you have a job or when you don't?

160. Which would you prefer to be – incredibly successful at work with a poor private life, or very happy in your private life with an only marginally acceptable working life?

161. Who would be the person in your organization you would most like to sit down and talk to? What ten questions would you like to ask them?

162. Would it be important or matter to you if your spouse or partner was more successful in their career than you were?

163. What do you look for in your ideal manager?

164. Who are the most difficult people you work with? What does it say about you and what are the implications for your career?

165. Who would you prefer to be appraised by:

- your boss?
- your colleagues?
- your subordinates?

Why?

166. Which is better, a career with a poor start and a good finish or a good start and a poor finish? Which of these career tracks do you appear to be on?

167. At meetings at work, do you tend to speak more than you listen or listen more than you speak?

168. Do friends made through work tend to become your social friends or do you keep these two aspects of your life separate?

169. If you wrote a mission statement for yourself, what would you say?

170. What does the state of your office/workstation say about you? Should you be making some changes?

171. Why would you employ yourself? Why wouldn't you?

172. What are your current career objectives? (Are they SMART = specific, measurable, attainable, realistic and time bound?)

173. How did your family influence your career and do these influences still apply?

174. Have you ever asked for a rise in pay or a promotion? Why or why not?

175. What are going to be the future skills and requirements of your job?

176. Identify six reasons why your employer should want to continue to employ you?

177. How are you keeping up-to-date in your chosen field? How much reading do you need to do and how will you make time to do it?

178. If a friend at work confided in you that he or she had AIDS, would you feel duty bound to let your employer know? Would your relationship with that person change?

179. What do you look for in your ideal subordinate?

180. What would you do if you discovered that your boss's boss was sexually harassing a colleague? Would it make any difference if the colleague did not know that you knew?

181. In your career do you want to wear out or to rust out?

182. What prevents you from doing what you want? Do you have mainly external or internal constraints?

183. What are going to be the major technological influences on your job and career in the next five years?

184. If you were telephoned by a head-hunter today who wanted to put you on the agency's register, how specific could you be about the next job you wanted and how much you would be prepared to move for?

185. What makes you change jobs? (Does the initiative lie with you or others?)

186. If you were to be appraised this week for the past year's work, what would your appraiser say and what would be the implications for your future?

187. What were your favourite subjects at school and how do they relate to or support your current work?

188. Who is the best at doing what you do, who is the best at doing what you want to do and how can you be like them?

189. Identify four reasons why an employer would not hire you for your next job and what are you going to do about them?

190. If you were to be granted a sabbatical year next year with your time to be spent in some way related to your work, what would you do or study, and who would you like to meet or interview?

191. When did you last discuss your career plans with your family and those who are important to you? Should those who are close to you be privy to your plans?

192. Are you more forgiving with colleagues and subordinates than you are with your family?

193. What is the biggest contribution you can make to your present organization?

194. Why have you been selected for promotion in the past?

195. What is stopping you from pursuing your career goals? And what is your plan for these blocks?

196. Do you believe in luck and good fortune, or do you think that people have to make their own luck?

197. How hard are you prepared to work to achieve your career goals? How hard do you actually work for your goals?

198. How can you be more positive about:

- yourself at work?
- your job?
- your boss?
- your product or service?
- your organization?

199. With whom are you having difficulties at work and what can you do to improve your relationship?

200. If you were to start your career all over again, what would you change and why?

20 QUESTIONS TO ASK YOURSELF WHEN CONSIDERING TAKING A NEW JOB

1. Can I do the job on offer?

2. Do I want the job on offer?

3. How does the job fit into my career plans?

4. What are the prospects like for my development?

5. Will I be able to work well with my boss?

6. Do the values and culture of this organization match my own?

7. What are the success criteria for the job? Are they realistic? And can I achieve them?

8. Have I, or can I get sufficient resources to do what I have to do?

9. What happened to the previous job holder – if there wasn't one, how did the job come about?

10. Why am I being offered this position – what skills and experience make me the right candidate?

11. How will the job help me in developing skills and career experience?

12. Would those whose views I value be proud of me if I told them about this job?

13. What is the standing of the organization within its sector?

14. What are going to be the major challenges in the job?

15. What makes this organization stand out from its competitors?

16. How long should I stay in this job?

17. Can I make an immediate contribution in this job and quickly establish the right reputation for myself?

18. Is there sufficient executive power in the job to match the responsibilities?

19. Why do I really want this job?

20. Will I be paid my true market worth?

FURTHER ASSISTANCE

Max Eggert is available to speak at conventions, to consult with organisations and work with individuals on career development matters. For information on products, services and programmes, or if you have any questions about this or any of his other books, please write to him at any of the following addresses:

Suite 202
Level 2
71 York Street
Sydney 2000
NSW
Australia

94 High Street
Lindfield
West Sussex RH16 2HP
England

10 Bracken Drive
Dunston
Gateshead
Tyne & Wear NE11 9QP
England